MW00848556

THE DELPHIC MAXIMS

Warbler Press

www.warblerpress.com

© Warbler Press 2020

All rights reserved.

Printed in the United States of America with chlorine-free ink on acid-free interior paper made from 30% post-consumer waste recycled material supplied by a Forest Stewardship Council-certified provider.

ISBN 978-1-7345881-0-1 (paperback)
ISBN 978-1-7345881-1-8 (e-book)

THE DELPHIC MAXIMS

147 ANCIENT RULES FOR A HAPPY LIFE

The foundation of Delphi occurred before recorded history. Three early writers describe its origins: the author of the *Homeric Hymn to Apollo*, Aeschylus, and Euripides. From them we know that the Temple at Delphi was a place of worship for Gaia (Ge), the Earth goddess.

According to the *Homeric Hymn*, the god Apollo "went about the earth seeking a place of oracle for men" and determined to take possession of Pytho (Delphi) for this purpose. He did so by slaying Python, the dragon that guarded the area. Then, in the guise of a dolphin, he leapt aboard a Cretan ship, and forced the crew to serve him. Pytho was then renamed Delphi after the dolphin *(delphis)* and the cult of Apollo displaced the worship of Gaia in the 8th c. B.C.

Apollo's medium was Pythia, a high priestess who, under his inspiration, was thought to have delivered the oracles. Later, the 5th c. B.C. scholar Stobaeus credited the 147 Greek maxims inscribed at Delphi to the Seven Sages of Greece (leading philosophers and politicians) who gathered at Delphi in the early 6th c. B.C. to form a code of ethical maxims.

Their selection was inscribed on columns in front of Apollo's temple, thereby publishing the official text. The maxims were used throughout the Greek world until the fall of the Byzantine Empire in 1453 A.D.

There is no definitive translation of the Greek maxims and even ancient Greeks had difficulty understanding some of the more archaic commandments. This edition is based on a compilation of historical and authoritative English translations and scholarly commentary.

THE DELPHIC MAXIMS
are a set of 147
precepts inscribed at the
Temple of Apollo at Delphi
in the sixth century B.C.
They were at first commonly
attributed to Apollo's high
priestess, the Oracle at
Delphi, and later to the
Seven Sages of Greece.
Contemporary scholars
believe that the maxims
originated as popular
proverbs that, even long
before they were formalized,
shaped the foundation of
Greek society.

1
Follow God

Ἔπου θεῷ

2
Obey the law
Νόμῳ πείθου

3
Worship the Gods
Θεοὺς σέβου

4
Respect your parents
Γονεῖς αἰδοῦ

5
Be overcome by justice
Ἡττῶ ὑπὸ δικαίου

6
Know what you have learned
Γνῶθι μαθών

7
Perceive what you have heard
Ἀκούσας νόει

8
Know yourself
Σαυτὸν ἴσθι

9
Intend to get married
Γαμεῖν μέλλε

10
Know your opportunity
Καιρὸν γνῶθι

11
Think as a mortal
Φρόνει θνητά

12

If you are a stranger act like one

Ξένος ὢν ἴσθι

13
Honor the hearth
Ἑστίαν τίμα

14
Control yourself
Ἄρχε σεαυτοῦ

15
Help your friends
Φίλοις βοήθει

16
Control anger
Θυμοῦ κράτει

17

Exercise prudence

Φρόνησιν ἄσκει

18

Honor providence

Πρόνοιαν τίμα

19

Do not use an oath

Ὅρκῳ μὴ χρῶ

20
Love friendship
Φιλίαν ἀγάπα

21
Cling to discipline
Παιδείας ἀντέχου

22
Pursue a good reputation
Δόξαν δίωκε

23
Seek wisdom
Σοφίαν ζήλου

24
Praise the good

Καλὸν εὖ λέγε

25

Find fault with no one

Ψέγε μηδένα

26
Praise virtue

Ἐπαίνει ἀρετήν

27
Practice what is just

Πρᾶττε δίκαια

28
Be kind to friends

Φίλοις εὐνόει

29
Watch out for your enemies
Ἐχθροὺς ἀμύνου

30
Exercise nobility of character

Εὐγένειαν ἄσκει

31
Shun evil

Κακίας ἀπέχου

32
Be impartial
Κοινὸς γίνου

33
Guard what is yours
Ἴδια φύλαττε

34
Shun what belongs to others
Ἀλλοτρίων ἀπέχου

35
Listen to everyone
Ἄκουε πάντα

36
Be (religiously) silent
Εὔφημος ἴσθι

37
Do a favor for a friend
Φίλῳ χαρίζου

38
Nothing to excess
Μηδὲν ἄγαν

39
Use time economically
Χρόνου φείδου

40
Foresee the future
Ὅρα τὸ μέλλον

41
Despise insolence
Ὕβριν μίσει

42
Have respect for suppliants
Ἱκέτας αἰδοῦ

43
Accommodate yourself
to everything

Πᾶσιν ἁρμόζου

44
Educate your sons
Υἱοὺς παίδευε

45
Give what you have
Ἔχων χαρίζου

46
Fear deceit
Δόλον φοβοῦ

47

Speak well of everyone

Εὐλόγει πάντας

48

Be a seeker of wisdom

Φιλόσοφος γίνου

49

Choose what is divine

Ὅσια κρῖνε

50
Act when you know
Γνοὺς πρᾶττε

51
Shun murder

Φόνου ἀπέχου

52

Wish for things possible

Εὔχου δυνατά

53

Consult the wise

Σοφοῖς χρῶ

54

Test the character of a person

Ἦθος δοκίμαζε

55
Give back what you have received
Λαβὼν ἀπόδος

56
Look down on no one
Ὑφορῶ μηδένα

57
Use your skill

Τέχνη χρῶ

58
Do what you mean to do
Ὅ μέλλεις, δός

59

Honor a benefaction

Εὐεργεσίας τίμα

60

Be jealous of no one

Φθόνει μηδενί

61

Be on your guard

Φυλακῇ πρόσεχε

62
Praise hope
Ἐλπίδα αἴνει

63
Despise slander
Διαβολὴν μίσει

64
Gain possessions justly
Δικαίως κτῶ

65
Honor good men
Ἀγαθοὺς τίμα

66
Know the judge
Κριτὴν γνῶθι

67
Master wedding-feasts
Γάμους κράτει

68
Recognize fortune
Τύχην νόμιζε

69
Flee a pledge
Ἐγγύην φεῦγε

70
Speak plainly
Ἁπλῶς διαλέγου

71
Associate with your peers

Ὁμοίοις χρῶ

72

Govern your expenses

Δαπανῶν ἄρχου

73

Be happy with what you have

Κτώμενος ἥδου

74

Revere a sense of shame

Αἰσχύνην σέβου

75

Fulfill a favor

Χάριν ἐκτέλει

76

Pray for happiness

Εὐτυχίαν εὔχου

77

Be fond of fortune

Τύχην στέργε

78
Observe what you have heard

Ἀκούων ὅρα

79

Work for what you can own

Ἐργάζου κτητά

80
Despise strife
Ἔριν μίσει

81
Detest disgrace
Ὄνειδος ἔχθαιρε

82
Restrain the tongue

Γλῶτταν ἴσχε

83
Keep yourself from insolence
Ὕβριν ἀμύνου

84
Make just judgments
Κρῖνε δίκαια

85
Use what you have
Χρῶ χρήμασιν

86
Judge incorruptibly
Ἀδωροδόκητος δίκαζε

87
Accuse one who is present
Αἰτιῶ παρόντα

88
Speak only when you know
Λέγε εἰδώς

89
Do not depend on strength
Βίας μὴ ἔχου

90

Live without sorrow

Ἀλύπως βίου

91

Live together meekly

Ὁμίλει πρᾴως

92

Finish the race without
shrinking back

Πέρας ἐπιτέλει μὴ ἀποδειλιῶν

93
Deal kindly with everyone
Φιλοφρόνει πᾶσιν

94

Do not curse your sons

Υἱοῖς μὴ καταρῶ

95

Guide your wife

Γυναικὸς ἄρχε

96

Benefit yourself

Σεαυτὸν εὖ ποίει

97

Be courteous

Εὐπροσήγορος γίνου

98
Give a timely response
Ἀποκρίνου ἐν καιρῷ

99
Struggle with glory
Πόνει μετ᾽ εὐκλείας

100
Act decisively
Πρᾶττε ἀμετανοήτως

101
Repent when you err

Ἁμαρτάνων μετανόει

102
Control the eye
Ὀφθαλμοῦ κράτει

103
Give a timely counsel
Βουλεύου χρόνῳ

104
Act quickly
Πρᾶττε συντόμως

105
Guard friendship
Φιλίαν φύλαττε

106
Be grateful
Εὐγνώμων γίνου

107

Pursue harmony

Ὁμόνοιαν δίωκε

108

Do not reveal secrets

Ἄρρητον κρύπτε

109

Fear ruling

Τὸ κρατοῦν φοβοῦ

110
Pursue what is profitable
Τὸ συμφέρον θηρῶ

111

Accept due measure

Καιρὸν προσδέχου

112

Do away with enmities

Ἔχθρας διάλυε

113
Accept old age
Γῆρας προσδέχου

114

Do not boast in might

Ἐπὶ ῥώμῃ μὴ καυχῶ

115

Speak respectfully

Εὐφημίαν ἄσκει

116

Flee enmity

Ἀπέχθειαν φεῦγε

117
Acquire wealth justly
Πλούτει δικαίως

118
Do not abandon honor
Δόξαν μὴ λεῖπε

119
Despise evil
Κακίαν μίσει

120
Venture into danger prudently
Κινδύνευε φρονίμως

121

Do not tire of learning

Μανθάνων μὴ κάμνε

122

Do not cease to be thrifty

Φειδόμενος μὴ λεῖπε

123
Admire oracles
Χρησμοὺς θαύμαζε

124
Love whom you rear
Οὓς τρέφεις, ἀγάπα

125
Do not oppose someone absent
Ἀπόντι μὴ μάχου

126
Respect an elder
Πρεσβύτερον αἰδοῦ

127

Teach a youngster

Νεώτερον δίδασκε

128

Do not trust wealth

Πλούτῳ ἀπίστει

129
Respect yourself
Σεαυτὸν αἰδοῦ

130
Do not begin to be insolent
Μὴ ἄρχε ὑβρίζειν

131
Honor your ancestors
Προγόνους στεφάνου

132
Die for your country
Θνῆσκε ὑπὲρ πατρίδος

133

Do not be discontented by life

Τῷ βίῳ μὴ ἄχθου

134
Do not make fun of the dead
Ἐπὶ νεκρῷ μὴ γέλα

135

Share the load of the unfortunate

Ἀτυχοῦντι συνάχθου

136

Gratify without harming

Χαρίζου ἀβλαβῶς

137
Grieve for no one
Μὴ ἐπὶ παντὶ λυποῦ

138
Beget by noble means
Ἐξ εὐγενῶν γέννα

139
Make promises to no one
Ἐπαγγέλλου μηδενί

140
Do not wrong the dead

Φθιμένους μὴ ἀδίκει

141

Be well off as a mortal

Εὖ πάσχε ὡς θνητός

142

Do not trust fortune

Τύχῃ μὴ πίστευε

143

As a child be well-behaved

Παῖς ὢν κόσμιος ἴσθι

144

as a youth be self-disciplined

ἡβῶν ἐγκρατής

145

in middle-age be just

μέσος δίκαιος

146

as an old man be sensible

πρεσβύτης εὔλογος

147

on reaching the end be
without sorrow

τελευτῶν ἄλυπος

SOURCES

Anonymous. *Hesiod: The Homeric Hymns and Homerica* with an English Translation by Hugh G. Evelyn-White. *Homeric Hymns*. London, William Heinemann Ltd.; New York: The MacMillion Co., 1914.

Bowden, Hugh. *Classical Athens and the Delphic Oracle: Divination and Democracy*. Cambridge: Cambridge University Press, 2005.

Broad, William J. *The Oracle: Ancient Delphi and the Science Behind its Lost Secrets*. New York: Penguin Press, 2006.

Fontenrose, Joseph Eddy. *The Delphic Oracle, Its Responses and Operations, with a Catalogue of Responses*, Berkeley: University of California Press, 1987.

Fontenrose, Joseph Eddy. *Python: A Study of the Delphic Myth and its Origin*. Berkeley: University of California Press, 1980.

Guthrie, W. K. C. *The Greeks and their Gods*. London: Methuen, 1950.

Meineke, August. *Ioannis Stobaei Florilegium*, Volume 3, Leipzig: B. G. Teubner, 1856.

Oikonomides, A.N. 'Records of "The Commandments of the Seven Wise Men" in the 3rd century B.C.', Chicago: *Classical Bulletin*, Vol. 63, 1987.

Parke, Herbert William. *A History of the Delphic Oracle*. Oxford: Basil Blackwell, 1939.

Parke, Herbert William. *The Delphic Oracle*. Oxford: Basil Blackwell, 1956.

Poulson, Frederick. *Delphi*. London: Gyldendal, 1920.

Schuré, Edouard. *Pythagoras and the Delphic Mysteries*. London: Wm. Rider & Son, Ltd. 1923.

Sikelianos, Angelos. *The Delphic Word*. New York: H. Vinal, 1928.

Wilkins, Eliza Gregory. *The Delphic Maxims in Literature*. Chicago: University of Chicago Press, 1929.

Made in the USA
Las Vegas, NV
27 November 2023

81630635R00062